PHONICS: GRADE 2
TABLE OF CONTENTS

PHONICS – GRADE 2

This book is designed to review phonics to enhance reading ability. The activities provide a fun way to reinforce daily learning and will keep skills sharp over an extended vacation, as well as allow a child to gain an edge from extra practice.

ORGANIZATION

These activities are designed to reinforce skills that are important for beginning readers. This book is divided into four sections: *Letters and Sounds: Consonants; Letters and Sounds: Vowels; Letters and Sounds: Consonant Blends;* and *Letters and Sounds: Consonant Digraphs.* Each section focuses on a single concept, and review pages appear periodically to give children the opportunity to work with several familiar sound/letter patterns while they learn new ones.

- **Letters and Sounds: Consonants** In this section, children will review listening for and writing consonants in initial, final, and medial positions.

- **Letters and Sounds: Vowels** The activities in this section will help children review the short and long sounds that vowels represent. Children will progress from listening for and writing vowels to reading sentences and stories with long and short vowel words.

- **Letters and Sounds: Consonant Blends** The activities in this section will help children recognize the sounds that consonant blends represent. Children will progress from listening for and writing consonant blends to reading sentences and stories with consonant blend words.

- **Letters and Sounds: Consonant Digraphs** The activities for consonant digraphs follow the same pattern as the consonant blend pages.

USE

This book is designed for independent use by students who have been introduced to letters and sounds. Copies of the activities can be given to individuals, pairs of students, or small groups for completion. They may be used as a center activity. If students are familiar with the content, the worksheets can also be used as homework.

To begin, determine the implementation which fits your students' needs and your classroom structure. The following plan suggests a format for this implementation:

1. **Explain** the purpose of the worksheets to your class. Let students know that these activities will be fun as well as helpful.

2. **Review** the mechanics of how you want students to work with the activities. Do you want them to work in groups? Are these activities for homework?

3. **Introduce** students to the process and to the purpose of the activities. Go over the directions. Work with children when they have difficulty. Work only a few pages at a time to avoid pressure.

4. **Do** a practice activity together.

ADDITIONAL NOTES

1. **Parent Communication** Sign the *Letter to Parents* and send it home with students.

2. **Bulletin Board** Display completed activities to show student progress.

3. **By ME! Books** There are four child-sized books for children to make. Have children color the illustrations and complete the activity. To turn the page into a book, children first fold the page in the middle. Then they fold it again, making sure the cover is on top.

4. **Assessment Test** On pages 5 and 6 is an Assessment Test. You can use the test as a diagnostic tool by administering it before children begin the activities. After children have completed the lessons, let them retake it to see the progress they have made.

5. **Center Activities** Use the worksheets as center activities to give students the opportunity to work cooperatively.

6. **Have fun** Working with these activities can be fun as well as meaningful for you and your students.

ANSWER KEY TO ASSESSMENT TEST

Name _____ Date _____

Test Yourself

Name each picture. Fill in the circle next to the letters that stand for the missing blend. Write the letters to complete the words.

○ st ○ nd ● mp st**mp**	○ sl ● sk ○ sp sk unk	○ br ○ bl ● tr tr ee
● pl ○ sp ○ spl pl ant	○ scr ○ cl ● spr spring	○ gl ● fl ○ str fl ag
○ sw ● tw ○ sn tw ins	○ sk ○ cr ● nd han**d**	● gr ○ fr ○ sm grill
● squ ○ spr ○ spl square	● sw ○ dr ○ squ swing	○ sm ○ nt ● sp wa**sp**

© Steck-Vaughn Company   5   Assessment Test   Phonics 2: Decoding, SV 6798-0

Name _____ Date _____

Test Yourself

Read each sentence. Fill in the circle next to the word that completes the sentence.

1. Take a seat on the park _____.	● bench ○ wrench ○ bank
2. Shelly _____ a thank-you note.	● wrote ○ road ○ white
3. The _____ made a big splash in the water.	● whale ○ wink ○ know
4. When do you think the _____ will hatch?	○ thick ○ shack ● chick
5. Rice and _____ are good to eat.	○ fence ● corn ○ cup
6. It is fun to sail a _____ on the lake.	○ bat ○ bone ● boat
7. Mom will honk the car _____ when she gets here.	● horn ○ hurt ○ hat
8. A _____ cub does not make a good pet.	○ cot ○ cut ● cute

© Steck-Vaughn Company   6   Assessment Test   Phonics 2: Decoding, SV 6798-0

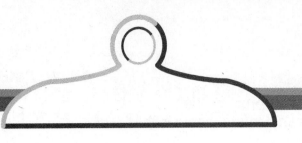

Dear Parent,

     During this school year, our class will be learning phonics to prepare for reading. We will be completing activity sheets that provide practice with these reading readiness skills. Learning to read can be stressful. By working together to prepare the students, we can reduce their stress level and help them learn that reading is fun.

     From time to time, I may send home activity sheets. To best help your child, please consider the following suggestions:

- Provide a quiet place to work.
- Go over the directions together.
- Encourage your child to do his or her best.
- Check the lesson when it is complete.
- Go over your child's work, and note improvements as well as problems.

     Help your child maintain a positive attitude about the activities. Let your child know that each lesson provides an opportunity to have fun and to learn. Above all, enjoy this time you spend with your child. As your child's ability to read develops, he or she will feel your support.

     Thank you for your help!

                       Cordially,

Name _____ Date _____

Test Yourself

Name each picture. Fill in the circle next to the letters that stand for the missing blend. Write the letters to complete the words.

○ st ○ nd ○ mp **sta__**	○ sl ○ sk ○ sp **__unk**	○ br ○ bl ○ tr **__ee**
○ pl ○ sp ○ spl **__ant**	○ scr ○ cl ○ spr **__ing**	○ gl ○ fl ○ str **__ag**
○ sw ○ tw ○ sn **__ins**	○ sk ○ cr ○ nd **ha__**	○ gr ○ fr ○ sm **__ill**
○ squ ○ spr ○ spl **__are**	○ sw ○ dr ○ squ **__ing**	○ sm ○ nt ○ sp **wa__**

Test Yourself

Read each sentence. Fill in the circle next to the word that completes the sentence.

1. Take a seat on the park _____.	○ bench ○ wrench ○ bank
2. Shelly _____ a thank-you note.	○ wrote ○ road ○ white
3. The _____ made a big splash in the water.	○ whale ○ wink ○ know
4. When do you think the _____ will hatch?	○ thick ○ shack ○ chick
5. Rice and _____ are good to eat.	○ fence ○ corn ○ cup
6. It is fun to sail a _____ on the lake.	○ bat ○ bone ○ boat
7. Mom will honk the car _____ when she gets here.	○ horn ○ hurt ○ hat
8. A _____ cub does not make a good pet.	○ cot ○ cut ○ cute

Name _____ Date _____

Hear First Sounds

Say each picture name. Circle the letter that stands for the **first** sound.

n / m / r	y / w / z	t / l / d
y / w / v	g / qu / p	d / b / h
x / w / y	c / g / qu	k / h / b
s / k / z	s / f / t	m / h / r
n / r / qu	w / y / v	n / k / h

Write First Sounds

Say each picture name. Write the letter that stands for the **first** sound.

_____	_____	_____
_____	_____	_____
_____	_____	_____
_____	_____	_____
_____	_____	_____

Write First Sounds

Say each picture name. Write the letter that stands for the **first** sound.

___	___	___
___	___	___
___	___	___
___	___	___
___	___	___

Hear Last Sounds

Say each picture name. Circle the letter that stands for the **last** sound.

d k l	d b h	m n r
s x z	h n t	g t p
g q x	b k d	p x y
l t f	b g p	t f s
d m w	w z v	t h l

Write Last Sounds

Say each picture name. Write the letter that stands for the **last** sound.

goat ___	door ___	drum ___
dog ___	hook ___	ship ___
bus ___	pail ___	fox ___
crib ___	ant ___	house ___
bed ___	sun ___	bug ___

Hear and Write Middle Sounds

Say each picture name. Write the letter that stands for the **middle** sound.

bea __ er

ca __ in

li __ ard

me __ al

ro __ in

pa __ er

sa __ ad

ca __ oe

pa __ ade

wa __ on

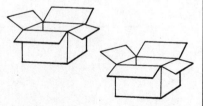

bo __ es

wo __ an

www.svschoolsupply.com

© Steck-Vaughn Company

Medial Consonant Sounds

Phonics 2: Decoding, SV 6798-0

Name _____ Date _____

Hear and Write Middle Sounds

Say each picture name. Write the letter that stands for the **middle** sound.

ca __ el	ba __ on	ro __ ot

wi __ er	gui __ ar	sho __ el
		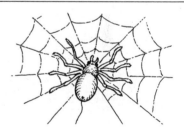
fo __ es	ra __ or	spi __ er

ti __ er	ru __ er	ri __ er

Medial Consonant Sounds

Phonics 2: Decoding, SV 6798-0

Missing Letters

Say each picture name. Write the letter that stands for the **missing** sound.

 lea__	 __ey	 __ueen
 __awn	 a__	 pa__ade
 li__ard	 __eep	 bu__
 ro__ot	 boo__	 __at

Consonant Sounds Review

Phonics 2: Decoding, SV 6798-0

Name _____ Date _____

Missing Letters

Say each picture name. Write the letters that stand for the **first**, **middle**, and **last** sounds.

__ i __ e __	__ a __ a __	__ __ a __ e __
__ a __ e __	__ a __ o	__ a __ o __
__ a __ o __	__ ea __ e __	__ o __ e __
__ __ o __ i	__ o __ a __	__ i __ e __

Consonant Sounds Review

Phonics 2: Decoding, SV 6798-0

Match Pictures and Sentences

Circle the sentence that tells about the picture.

I. Rex sees a bug.

Rex sees a tub.

Rex sees a bone.

---

2. Rex hides.

Rex hops.

Rex eats.

---

3. Pam gets wet.

Pam gets Rex.

Pam sits.

---

4. Rex is in a pen.

Rex is dry.

Rex is wet.

---

5. Rex gets a bed.

Rex gets a prize.

Rex gets a coat.

Name _____ Date _____

Riddles

Circle the word that names the picture. Write it on the line.

I. Is it a **fox**, **box**, or an **ox**?		_____
2. Is it a **cap**, **cat**, or **cab**?		_____
3. Is it a **dog**, **hog**, or **log**?		_____
4. Is it a **can**, **pan**, or **van**?		_____
5. Is it a **wig**, **pig**, or **dig**?		_____
6. Is it a **pen**, **pet**, or **peg**?		_____
7. Is it a **bug**, **bus**, or **bun**?		_____
8. Is it **men**, **ten**, or a **hen**?		_____

Consonant Sounds in Context

Phonics 2: Decoding, SV 6798-0

Name _____ Date _____

Classifying

Circle the words that belong.

I. Which are things to ride?	
van jeep keep	
like tan bike	
2. Which are things to eat?	
run meat lake	
cake bun seat	
3. Which are things that grow?	
cub mud cup	
pup tub bud	
4. Which are ways to move?	
fog run hop	
top jog bun	
5. Which are in the sky?	
soon car fun	
sun moon star	
6. Which live on a farm?	
hen wig goat	
coat ten pig	

www.svschoolsupply.com

© Steck-Vaughn Company

Consonant Sounds in Context

Phonics 2: Decoding, SV 6798-0

Name _____ Date _____

Quiz Yourself

Name each picture. Write the letter that stands for the **missing** sound.

ra __ or	__ ay	bu __
roo __	__ ing	__ ueen
ri __ er	hoo __	__ ose
__ arn	fo __	ti __ er

Quiz Yourself

Phonics 2: Decoding, SV 6798-0

Quiz Yourself

Name each picture. Fill in the circle next to the letter that stands for the **missing** sound. Write the letter to complete the word.

○ g ○ b ○ k	○ f ○ t ○ l	○ b ○ p ○ d
ro__ot	lea__	__og
○ p ○ t ○ b	○ l ○ w ○ r	○ n ○ m ○ r
mo__	__ake	ha__
○ g ○ c ○ s	○ n ○ r ○ m	○ h ○ t ○ l
__oat	fa__	sa__ad
○ l ○ n ○ r	○ f ○ t ○ l	○ w ○ v ○ r
__ug	wa__er	__ig

Sounds of c

- When **c** is before **e, i,** or **y,** it can stand for the **s** sound in **sun.** Before other vowels, **c** usually stands for the **k** sound in **kite.**

cent   **c**at

Name the first picture in each row. Circle the pictures that have the same **c** sound as the first picture.

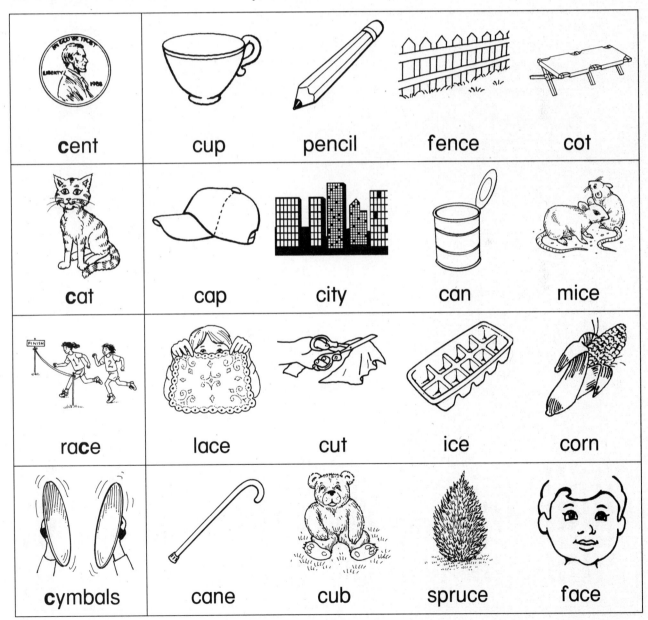

cent	cup	pencil	fence	cot
cat	cap	city	can	mice
ra**c**e	lace	cut	ice	corn
cymbals	cane	cub	spruce	face

Name _____ Date _____

A Trip to the City

Cecil goes to the city. Color the pictures that have the
c sound in **city**.

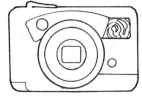

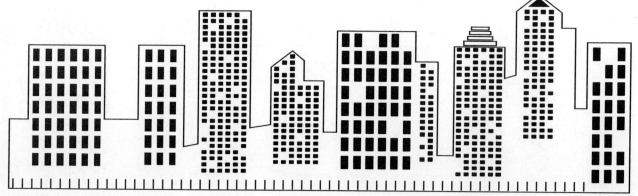

Variant Consonant **c**

Phonics 2: Decoding, SV 6798-0

Name _____ Date _____

Sounds and Sentences

Read each sentence. Circle the word that completes the sentence.
Write it on the line.

1. Cindy saved ten dollars and fifty _____.	cents cats
2. She wanted to spend it at the _____.	case circus
3. Cindy and Cecil rode in a _____.	cell cab
4. At one tent, they saw some bear _____.	cubs centers
5. The baby bears got up and _____.	laced danced
6. Then they saw a camel _____.	race mice
7. They tried cotton _____ for the first time.	candy ice
8. They hated to go back home to the _____.	car city

© Steck-Vaughn Company

Variant Consonant **c** in Context

Phonics 2: Decoding, SV 6798-0

Sounds of g

- When **g** is before **e, i,** or **y,** it can stand for the **j** sound in **jet**. The letters **dge** stand for the **j** sound, too.

gem   **g**as   ju**dge**

Name the first picture in each row. Circle the pictures that have the same **g** sound as the first picture.

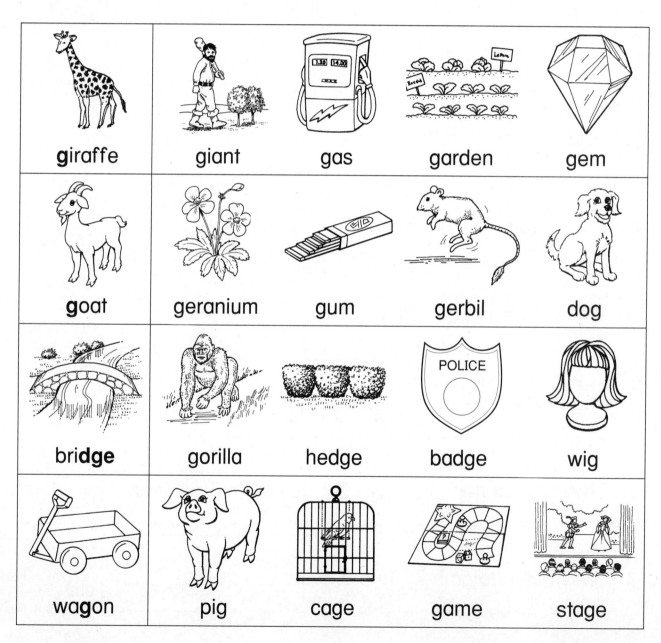

giraffe	**g**iant	**g**as	**g**arden	**g**em
goat	**g**eranium	**g**um	**g**erbil	dog
bri**dge**	**g**orilla	he**dge**	ba**dge**	wig
wa**g**on	pig	ca**g**e	**g**ame	sta**g**e

Name _____   Date _____

Word Game

Use the clues to write the words in the puzzle. Read down the letters in the box to answer the question.

stage	fudge	giant	goldfish
hedge	page	pig	gerbil

1. A big, big man ___ ___ ___ ___ ___

2. A farm animal that says "oink" ___ ___ ___

3. A small pet ___ ___ ___ ___ ___ ___

4. A part of a book ___ ___ ___ ___

5. A sweet candy ___ ___ ___ ___ ___

6. A pet that swims ___ ___ ___ ___ ___ ___ ___ ___

7. A fence made of plants ___ ___ ___ ___ ___

8. A place for a play ___ ___ ___ ___ ___

What are the tallest animals in the world?

___ ___ ___ ___ ___ ___ ___ ___

Variant Consonant **g**

Phonics 2: Decoding, SV 6798-0

Name _____ Date _____

Sounds and Sentences

Read each sentence. Circle the word that completes the sentence.
Write it on the line.

1. A _____ lives in the city.	game giant
2. He has a big, big _____ .	gate huge
3. He works out in a big, big _____ .	gym gum
4. His pet is a _____ .	giraffe hedge
5. One day the _____ came to visit.	general cage
6. She needed some _____ .	page gas
7. The giant _____ her some.	badge gave
8. "You are a _____ !" she said.	gem go

Sounds of s

- In **sun, s** stands for the **s** sound.
- In **rose, s** stands for the **z** sound.
- In **sugar, s** stands for the **sh** sound.

sun   ro**s**e   **s**ugar

Write **s, z,** or **sh** on the line to tell the sound that **s** stands for in each picture name.

soap _____   music _____   mi**ss**ion _____

bu**s** _____   ti**ss**ue _____   ho**s**e _____

sock _____   chee**s**e _____   **s**even _____

Name _____ Date _____

Sound Sort

Write each word from the box under the picture with the name that starts with the same **s** sound.

see	surely	music	us	gas
wise	tissue	please	side	his
nose	seven	mission	issue	sure

sun

rose

sugar

Variant Consonant **s**

Phonics 2: Decoding, SV 6798-0

Sounds and Sentences

Read each sentence. Circle the word that completes the sentence.
Write it on the line.

1. Sue _____ has a bad cold.	sun surely
2. Her _____ is all red.	song nose
3. It is as red as a _____.	mission rose
4. Sue needs more _____.	tissues hoses
5. _____ get her a new box.	Please This
6. Poor Sue! Is her throat _____, too?	sit sore
7. Sue can _____ a long rest.	use rise
8. I'm _____ that will cure her cold.	sugar sure

Match Pictures and Sentences

Read each sentence. Write the sentence that tells about the picture.

1. Carmen sees the giraffe.
   Carmen sees the geese.

_____

- - - - - - - - - - - - - - - - - -

_____

2. Sam has a rose garden.
   Sam soaps his car.

_____

- - - - - - - - - - - - - - - - - -

_____

3. Gina goes to the sea.
   Gina gets a pet gerbil.

_____

- - - - - - - - - - - - - - - - - -

_____

4. The goat hops over a fence.
   The goat eats the grass.

_____

- - - - - - - - - - - - - - - - - -

_____

Name _____ Date _____

Riddles

Circle the word that names the picture. Write it on the line.

1.	Is it a **stage**, a **page**, or **huge**?		_____
2.	Is it a **jar**, **car**, or **star**?		_____
3.	Is it a **gym**, **jam**, or **game**?	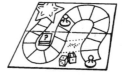	_____
4.	Is it a **judge**, **fudge**, or an **edge**?		_____
5.	Is it a **bus**, a **bug**, or **budge**?		_____
6.	Is it a **rose**, **hose**, or **nose**?		_____
7.	Is it the **sun**, **sugar**, or **sure**?		_____
8.	Is it **nice**, **dice**, or **mice**?		_____

Phonics 2: Decoding, SV 6798-0

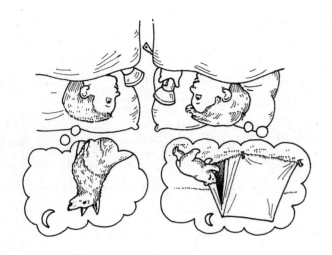

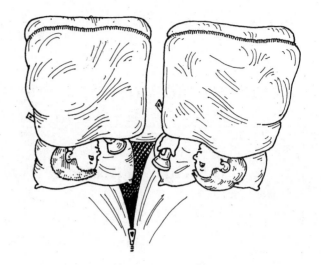

˙punos ɐ

in the back yard. They hear

George and Sam camp out

Is it a wild wolf?

Is it a bear cub?

The boys peek out. It is just a
_____
- -
_____ .

Camping Out

Finish the story. Tell what the
boys saw. Draw a picture.

_____

made this book!

Hear and Write Short a

Apple has the short **a** sound. Name each picture. If you hear the short **a** sound, as in **apple,** write **a** on the line.

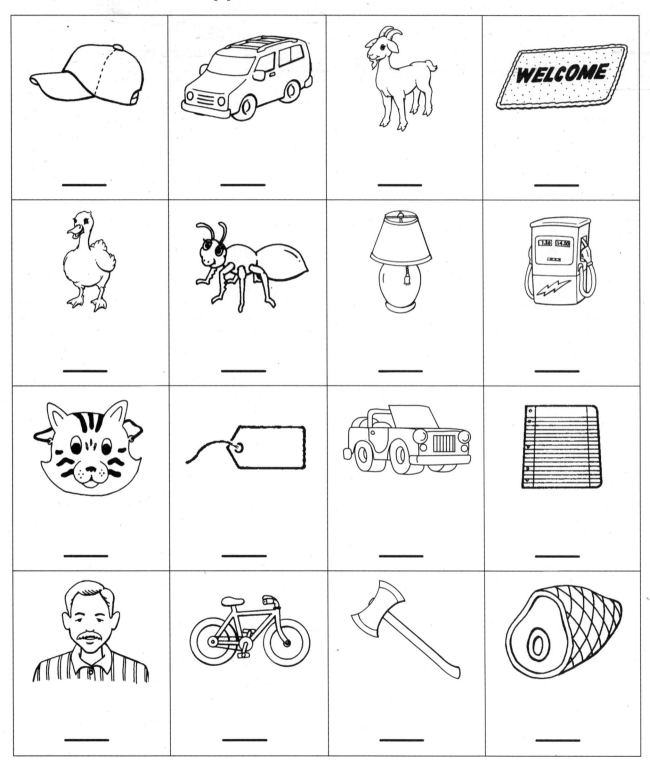

Match Words and Pictures

Read the short **a** words. Write the word that names each picture.

sat	cat	mat	bat	hat

tag	wag	rag	sag	bag

map	tap	lap	nap	cap

yam	dam	ram	ham	jam

fan	ran	can	man	pan

Name _____   Date _____

Hear and Write Short i

Pig has the short **i** sound. Name each picture. If you hear the short
i sound, as in **pig,** write **i** on the line.

Match Words and Pictures

Read the short **i** words. Write the word that names each picture.

will	ill	fill	hill	mill

_____

_____

kid	did	rid	lid	hid

_____

_____

hit	kit	bit	sit	fit

_____

_____

tin	pin	win	fin	bin

_____

_____

dig	pig	wig	fig	big

_____

_____

Phonics 2: Decoding, SV 6798-0

Hear and Write Short o

Ox has the short **o** sound. Name each picture. If you hear the short **o** sound, as in **ox,** write **o** on the line.

Match Words and Pictures

Read the short **o** words. Write the word that names each picture.

lock	mock	rock	sock	dock

_____

_____

cob	sob	job	rob	mob

_____

_____

box	fox	lox	ox	pox

_____

_____

cot	not	hot	dot	tot

_____

_____

hop	pop	mop	cop	top

_____

_____

www.svschoolsupply.com

© Steck-Vaughn Company

Short Vowel **o**

Phonics 2: Decoding, SV 6798-0

Hear and Write Short u

Umbrella has the short **u** sound. Name each picture. If you hear the short **u** sound, as in **umbrella,** write **u** on the line.

_____	_____	_____	_____
_____	_____	_____	_____
_____	_____	_____	_____
_____	_____	_____	_____

Name _____   Date _____

Match Words and Pictures

Read the short **u** words. Write the word that names each picture.

fun	run	gun	sun	bun

_____

_____

jug	hug	rug	dug	bug

_____

_____

hub	cub	tub	sub	rub

_____

_____

cut	but	rut	nut	hut

_____

_____

luck	duck	buck	tuck	puck

_____

_____

Hear and Write Short e

Nest has the short **e** sound. Name each picture. If you hear the short **e** sound, as in **nest,** write **e** on the line.

Match Words and Pictures

Read the short **e** words. Write the word that names each picture.

dent	went	rent	tent	cents

_____

_____

bell	well	sell	fell	yell

_____

_____

test	best	vest	west	nest

_____

_____

keg	leg	peg	egg	beg

_____

_____

yet	net	jet	pet	let

_____

_____

Phonics 2: Decoding, SV 6798-0

Name _____ Date _____

Short Vowel Review

Name the vowel and the first picture in each row. Color the pictures that have the same short vowel sound as the picture.

Name _____ Date _____

Mystery Vowel

Write the same vowel in each word to complete the sentence.

1. The d___cks had f___n in the wet m___d.

2. The c___t s___t on Tom's l___p.

3. A girl wants to g___t a p___t h___n.

4. The d___g h___ps ___n the l___g.

5. W___ll J___m's b___g f___sh w___n?

Short Vowel Review

Phonics 2: Decoding, SV 6798-0

Sounds and Sentences

Read each sentence. Circle the word that completes the sentence.
Write it on the line.

1. Jill can play the _____.	dress drums
2. She wants to start a _____.	band bun
3. She makes a list of _____.	pals pills
4. _____ of her pals can play.	Tan Ten
5. The pals _____ in with Jill.	sit sun
6. The band can play a _____.	six song
7. _____ claps his hands and taps his toe.	Dad Desk
8. The pals have a tip _____ band.	pet top

Match Pictures and Sentences

Circle the sentence that tells about the picture.

1. Sandy's hat fell.

A ball hits Sandy.

Sandy wants to get a hat.

2. Tess wants to sell a hat.

Tess sells pots and pans.

Tess sells hens and ducks.

3. Sandy sits on a cot.

Sandy puts on a hat.

Tess gets a big hat box.

4. The hat is big.

The hat has mud on it.

The hat is small.

5. It's fun to get a hat.

It's fun to get a hit.

It's fun to get a pup.

Hear Long a

• **Ax** has the short **a** sound.

• **Rake** has the long **a** sound.

Color the picture if its name has the long **a** sound.

cape

cap

game

bat

jay

cake

tape

pail

cane

vase

can

bag

Long Vowel a
Phonics 2: Decoding, SV 6798-0

Write Long a Words

• The letters **a_e, ai,** and **ay** can stand for the long **a** sound.

rake

rain

hay

Name each picture. Circle the picture name. Write the name.

gate gap	mail mall	hat hay
sat sail	tape tap	bat bait
nail nap	ran rain	mane man

Name _____   Date _____

Hear Long i

• **Pig** has the short **i** sound.

• **Kite** has the long **i** sound.

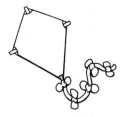

Color the picture if its name has the long **i** sound.

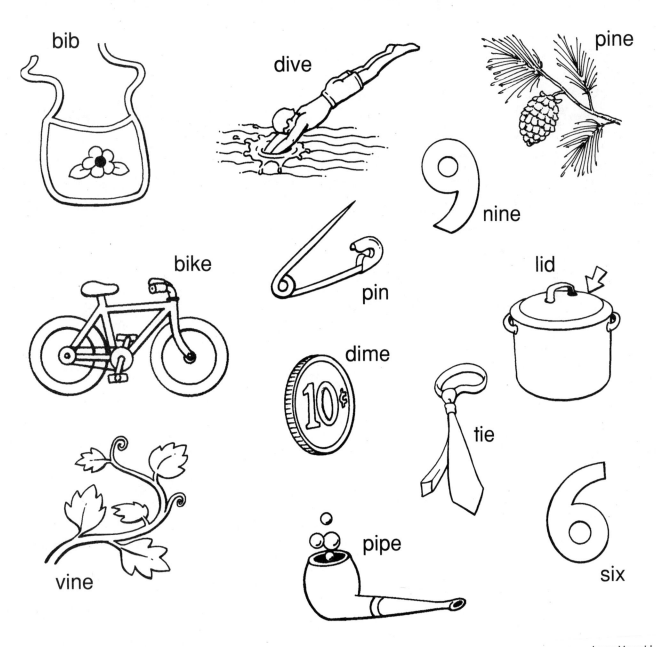

bib

dive

pine

bike

pin

nine

lid

dime

tie

six

vine

pipe

www.svschoolsupply.com

© Steck-Vaughn Company

Long Vowel **i**

Phonics 2: Decoding, SV 6798-0

Write Long i Words

- The letters **i_e** and **ie** can stand for the long **i** sound.

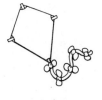

k**ite**

tie

Name each picture. Circle the picture name. Write the name.

dim / dime	his / hive	bit / bike
five / fin	pit / pie	dive / did
nip / nine	mice / mitt	win / vine

Name _____ Date _____

Hear Long o

- **Fox** has the short **o** sound.

- **Goat** has the long **o** sound.

Color the picture if its name has the long **o** sound.

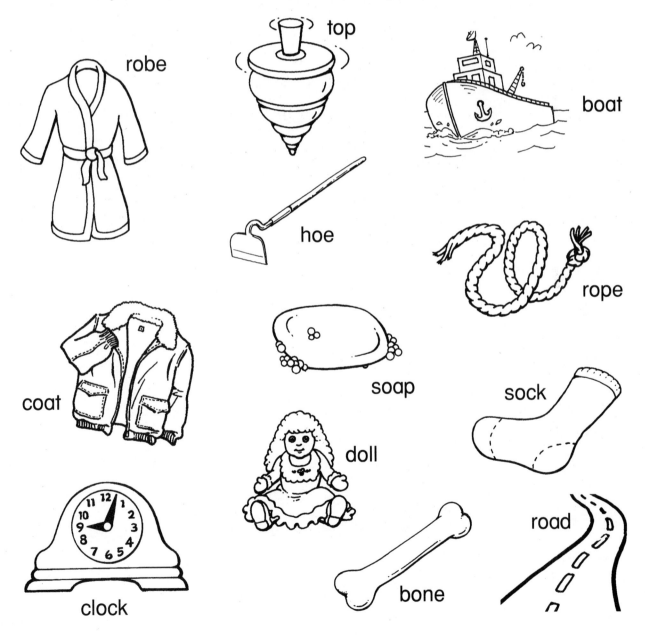

robe

top

boat

hoe

rope

coat

soap

sock

doll

clock

bone

road

Name _____ Date _____

Write Long o Words

• The letters **o_e**, **oa**, and **oe** can stand for the long **o** sound.

b**o**n**e**

g**oa**t

h**oe**

Name each picture. Circle the picture name. Write the name.

 cob cone	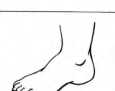 toad top	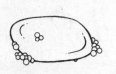 toe tot
soap sob	rob robe	home hop
dot doe	box boat	road rod

Name _____ Date _____

Hear Long u

- **Cub** has the short **u** sound.   - **Cube** has the long **u** sound.

Color the picture if its name has the long **u** sound.

tune

cup

mule

bug

June

ruler

duck

flute

tube

prune

fuse

sun

Name _____ **Date** _____

Write Long u Words

• The letters **u_e** can stand for the long **u** sound.

c**u**b**e**

Name each picture. Circle the picture name. Write the name.

plume / plum	flute / full	fumes / fun
Jud / June	mutt / mule	put / prune
dune / dust	fuss / fuse	tube / tub

Name _____ Date _____

Hear Long e

- **Bed** has the short **e** sound.

- **Beads** has the long **e** sound.

Color the picture if its name has the long **e** sound.

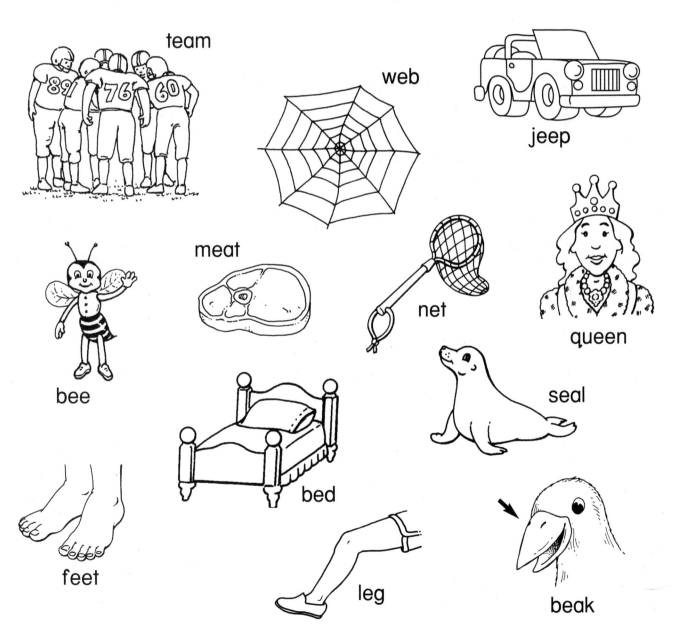

team

web

jeep

meat

net

queen

bee

bed

seal

feet

leg

beak

Write Long e Words

• The letters **ea** and **ee** can stand for the long **e** sound.

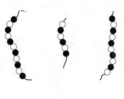   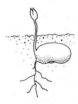

b**ea**d   s**ee**d

Name each picture. Circle the picture name. Write the name.

jet jeep	tea test	bed bee
_____	_____	_____
seal see	quest queen	meat met
_____	_____	_____
weed wed	peas pest	ten team
_____	_____	_____

Write Words with y as a Vowel

- At the end of a short word, like **fly, y** stands for the long **i** sound.
- At the end of a longer word, like **twenty, y** stands for the long **e** sound.

fly   twenty

Say and write each picture name. Write **y** to finish each word. Color the picture red if **y** has the vowel sound in **fly.** Color the picture green if **y** has the vowel sound in **twenty.**

sk_	happ_	cr_
sixt_	dr_	pupp_
fr_	bunn_	wh_

Name _____   Date _____

Sounds and Sentences

Read each sentence. Circle the word that completes the sentence.
Write it on the line.

1. What kind of pet would make you _____?	hay	happy
2. My pal Penny has _____ little fish.	twenty	try
3. Would you like a little _____?	bunny	boy
4. Maybe a _____ would please you.	puppy	pay
5. It would be fun to get a _____ kitten, too.	tray	tiny
6. _____ animals need extra care.	Baby	Bay
7. Some seem to _____ all the time.	cry	clay
8. They can be very _____, too.	say	sly

y as a Long Vowel

Phonics 2: Decoding, SV 6798-0

Name _____ Date _____

Long Vowel Review

Name the vowel and the first picture in each row. Color the pictures that have the same long vowel sound as the picture.

Name _____   Date _____

Write Long Vowel Words

Name each picture. Circle the picture name. Write the name.

met meat	tie toe	rain ran
cane can	free fry	got goat
kite kit	cube cub	wed weed
robe rob	plane plan	by bay

Phonics 2: Decoding, SV 6798-0

Name _____   Date _____

Match Pictures and Sentences

Read each sentence. Write the sentence that tells about the picture.

1. Bees like nice tiny buds.
   Bees are at home in a hive.

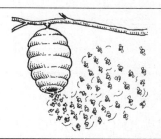

_____

- - - - - - - - - - - - - - - - - - -

_____

2. Jay can play the flute.
   Jay can use the hose.

_____

- - - - - - - - - - - - - - - - - - -

_____

3. The goat eats the rose.
   The baby mule is cute.

_____

- - - - - - - - - - - - - - - - - - -

_____

4. Dad will try to bake a lime pie.
   Dad cooks meat on the grill.

_____

- - - - - - - - - - - - - - - - - - -

_____

Story Time

Read the story. Choose the best title. Circle it and then write it on this line.

_____

- -

_____

"I made the team!" yelled Jean.

"Way to go," said Lee. "It will be fun to see you play ball."

Lee came to see Jean's game. As he sat in his seat, the ump yelled, "Play ball!"

"Hit a home run," screamed Lee. But Jean did not hit the ball.

"Strike one!" called the ump.

Jean looked at the sky. She hoped for rain. "Use your brain!" screamed Lee.

Jean tried her best. She waited for a good ball. When it came, Jean swung. She hit a home run.

"Safe at home," called the ump.

"Hooray for Jean," the team yelled. "They cannot beat us with Jean on the team."

A Long Fly Ball

Jean's Team Cannot Win

Jean Hits a Home Run

Name _____ Date _____

Quiz Yourself

Name each picture. Fill in the circle next to the letters that stand for the missing vowel sounds. Complete the names.

○ a ○ i ○ o b __ x	○ y ○ ee ○ u sk __	○ i ○ ai ○ o s __ l
○ u ○ u_e ○ ay m __ l __	○ e ○ ie ○ a v __ n	○ ea ○ y ○ e w __ b
○ u ○ o_e ○ a d __ ck	○ i_e ○ a_e ○ i f __ v __	○ y ○ ai ○ e bunn __
○ ie ○ ai ○ i h __ ll	○ oe ○ o ○ y h __	○ e ○ ee ○ u_e j __ p

Name _____ Date _____

Quiz Yourself

Read each sentence. Fill in the circle next to the word that completes the sentence.

1. Rob is going to _____ in a plane.	○ five ○ fly ○ face
2. It will be a long _____.	○ try ○ toe ○ trip
3. Grandma will _____ him at the end.	○ meet ○ mat ○ must
4. Rob has to _____.	○ pail ○ pack ○ pie
5. What will he _____?	○ tie ○ time ○ take
6. He will miss his _____.	○ puppy ○ web ○ lock
7. The trip is _____ days away.	○ fine ○ six ○ sock
8. He cannot wait to go up in the _____.	○ hat ○ sit ○ sky

www.svschoolsupply.com

© Steck-Vaughn Company

Quiz Yourself

Phonics 2: Decoding, SV 6798-0

Hear ar

Say each picture name. Listen for the **ar** sound in **car**.
Color the pictures that have the **ar** sound.

Hear or

Say each picture name. Listen for the **or** sound in **corn**.
Color the pictures that have the **or** sound.

Name _____ Date _____

Hear and Write ar and or

Name each picture. Write **ar** if you hear the same vowel sound as in **car**. Write **or** if you hear the same vowel sound as in **corn**.

p __ __ k	t __ __ ch	st __ __	p __ __ ch
y __ __ n	h __ __ p	h __ __ n	th __ __ n
st __ __ k	c __ __ k	b __ __ n	__ __ m

r-Controlled Vowels **ar** and **or**

Phonics 2: Decoding, SV 6798-0

Hear and Write ur, ir, and er

• The letters **ur, ir,** and **er** can stand for the same sound.

church

bird

herd

Write a word from the box to name each picture.

| nurse | purse | surf | girl | shirt | skirt | stir | twirl | fern |

<table>
<tr><td>

_ _ _ _ _ _ _ _ _ _

</td><td>

_ _ _ _ _ _ _ _ _ _

</td><td>

_ _ _ _ _ _ _ _ _ _

</td></tr>
<tr><td>

_ _ _ _ _ _ _ _ _ _

</td><td>

_ _ _ _ _ _ _ _ _ _

</td><td>

_ _ _ _ _ _ _ _ _ _

</td></tr>
<tr><td>

_ _ _ _ _ _ _ _ _ _

</td><td>

_ _ _ _ _ _ _ _ _ _

</td><td>

_ _ _ _ _ _ _ _ _ _

</td></tr>
</table>

Write Words with ar, or, ur, ir, and er

Name each picture. Circle the picture name. Write the name.

surf skirt	fork first	short shirt
germ girl	herd harm	burn barn
car cord	form fern	born bird
horn hurt	scarf star	church shark

Riddles

Write a word from the box to answer each riddle.

barn	fern	germ	hard
stork	girl	surf	twirl

1. It is not soft. What is it?

   _____

2. It can make you sick. What is it?

   _____

3. It is a big bird. What is it?

   _____

4. It is big waves by a beach. What is it?

   _____

5. You do this when you spin. What is it?

   _____

6. It is a home for a cow. What is it?

   _____

7. It is a green plant. What is it?

   _____

8. It is not a boy. What is it?

   _____

Name _____   Date _____

Classifying

Circle the words that belong.

1. Which are places?

barn	burn	church	park	pork
fort	fork	yard	yarn	born

2. Which are animals?

stork	start	short	shark	horse
horn	bird	lark	sharp	shirt

3. Which can you hear?

horn	snarl	harm	organ	harp
chirp	part	purr	smart	snort

4. Which are on a farm?

born	barn	horse	hard	corn
word	dirt	hard	dark	herd

5. Which can you wear?

sport	spur	shorts	storm	scarf
star	stern	shirt	fork	skirt

Letter Logic

Use the clues to find the mystery picture. Write the name of the picture on the line. Color the picture.

Hint: Cross out the pictures as you solve the clues.

mule   box   horn

leaf   pig   fern

It does **not** have a short vowel sound.

It does **not** end with **f.**

It does **not** start with **f.**

It is **not** the name of an animal.

It **does** have a vowel with **r.**

_____

It is _____.

Name _____ Date _____

Quiz Yourself

Read each sentence. Fill in the circle next to the word that completes the sentence.

I. Mort lives on a _____.	○ fern ○ farm ○ far
2. He grows _____.	○ churn ○ curls ○ corn
3. The _____ like the corn, too.	○ birds ○ barks ○ burns
4. Mort has cows and _____.	○ hurts ○ horns ○ horses
5. They need a clean _____.	○ born ○ barn ○ burr
6. Mort plants seeds in the _____.	○ dirt ○ darn ○ dart
7. He loads up his _____.	○ cord ○ cart ○ curl
8. At day's end, he rests on the _____.	○ porch ○ part ○ perk

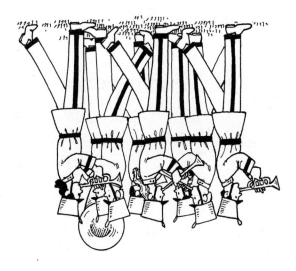

The band is on the march.
Joe plays a mean horn.
Lora plays the flute.

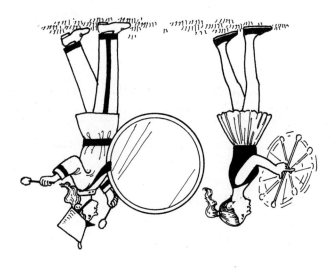

Jen beats her drum,
while Liz twirls and whirls.

And I play the
_____
— — — — — — — — — — — — —
_____ .

In the Band

_____
made this book!

Finish the story. Tell what you
want to play. Draw its picture.

Name _____ Date _____

Hear and Write s-Blends

Name each picture. Listen to the first part of the word. Write the first two letters.

skate   **sl**ide   **sm**ile   **sn**ail   **st**ar

Name _____   Date _____

Hear and Write s-Blends and tw

Name each picture. Listen to the first part of the word. Write the first two letters.

scale   **sp**ider   **sw**ing   **tw**elve

	20		
_____	_____	_____	_____

_____	_____	_____	_____
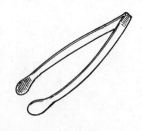			
_____	_____	_____	_____

www.svschoolsupply.com

© Steck-Vaughn Company

Initial **s**-Blends and **tw**

Phonics 2: Decoding, SV 6798-0

Name _____ Date _____

Write Words with s-Blends and tw

Name each picture. Circle the picture name. Write the name.

	smile slide		star scar		twins swans
	trip twig		stake snake		skunk spank
	twenty twist		swamp stamp		scale stale
	spider slide		spoon stone		swing sling

Name _____   Date _____

Hear and Write s-Blends with Three Letters

Name each picture. Listen to the first part of the word. Write the first three letters.

screen

split

spray

square

street

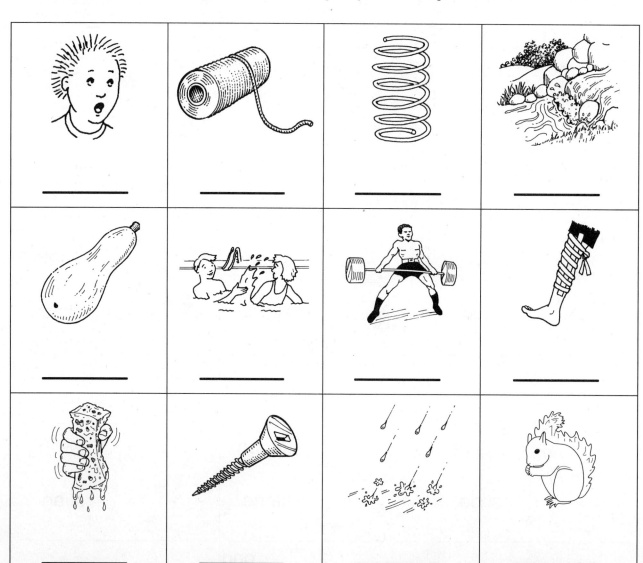

Name _____ Date _____

Sounds and Sentences

Read each sentence. Circle the word that completes the sentence.
Write it on the line.

1. It is fun to look at the _____.	sky scale split
2. In the dark, we see lots of _____.	stars squash springs
3. Those stars really _____.	startle splash sparkle
4. They seem to be on a big movie _____.	skate screen squash
5. If I _____, the stars seem to spin.	twin twirl twelve
6. The moon gives a _____ light, too.	strong spunk snip
7. Clouds over the moon look like _____.	smells smoke stops
8. I like to sit on the _____ and look up.	spoon string swing

Initial s-Blends and tw in Context

Phonics 2: Decoding, SV 6798-0

Name _____ Date _____

Match Pictures and Sentences

Read each sentence. Write the sentence that tells about the picture.

1. Mom sprays paint on the screen.
   The crew sprays stripes on the street.

_____

- -

_____

2. We like to skate in the city square.
   We like to splash in the city pool.

_____

- -

_____

3. Sharon smells a skunk.
   The skunk smells a rose.

_____

- -

_____

4. The team cannot score in the snow.
   The snowman has on Dad's scarf.

_____

- -

_____

Name _____ Date _____

Hear and Write r-Blends

Name each picture. Listen to the first part of the word. Write the first two letters.

bridge   **cr**ayon   **dr**agon   **fr**og

_____	_____	_____	_____
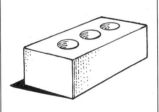			
_____	_____	_____	_____

_____	_____	_____	_____

www.svschoolsupply.com

© Steck-Vaughn Company

Initial **r**-Blends

Phonics 2: Decoding, SV 6798-0

Hear and Write r-Blends

Name each picture. Listen to the first part of the word. Write the first two letters.

grapes   **pr**ice   **tr**actor

Name _____ Date _____

Write Words with r-Blends

Name each picture. Circle the picture name. Write the name.

	raps grapes		bird brick		prize rise

	crab car		dorm drum		train rain

	frame farm		girl grill		rib crib

	drill dirt		fort fruit		turn truck

Initial r-Blends

Phonics 2: Decoding, SV 6798-0

Riddles

Write a word from the box to answer each riddle.

crab	drive	drum	green
frame	prize	train	trick

I. It is a water animal. It can pinch. What is it? _____

2. It is something you can win. What is it? _____

3. It rides on a track. What is it? _____

4. You do it to a car. What is it? _____

5. It is the name of a color. What is it? _____

6. It is a name for magic or a prank. What is it? _____

7. It's okay to hit this. It makes music. What is it? _____

8. You put a picture in this. What is it? _____

Name _____ Date _____

Sounds and Sentences

Read each sentence. Circle the word that completes the sentence. Write it on the line.

1. Brad wants to _____.	drip drive
2. He wants a big _____.	truck track
3. He could load it with _____.	bricks brought
4. He might load it with _____.	from fruit
5. Brad would use the _____ on hills.	bring brake
6. He would not skid on a wet _____.	bridge broom
7. He would _____ to be the best.	try tree
8. And he would never _____.	crash crown

Hear and Write l-Blends

Name each picture. Listen to the first part of the word. Write the first two letters.

block   **cl**ap   **fl**ag   **gl**ove   **pl**ate

 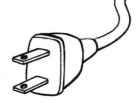  

_____   _____   _____   _____

_____   _____   _____   _____

_____   _____   _____   _____

Name _____   Date _____

Write Words with l-Blends

Name each picture. Circle the picture name. Write the name.

block flock	flag clog	clock blink
plus glass	flip plop	flap clap
plane glow	blue flute	flown clown
glum plum	black brick	clove globe

Name _____ Date _____

Riddles

Circle the word that names the picture. Write it on the line.

1. Is it a **block, box,** or **blob**?		_____
2. Is it a **fog, flip,** or **flag**?	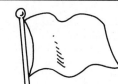	_____
3. Is it a **cloud, clown,** or **crown**?		_____
4. Is it a **play, pan,** or **plane**?		_____
5. Is it a **globe, grab,** or **glow**?		_____
6. Is it **gas, glaze,** or a **glass**?		_____
7. Is it **fall,** a **float,** or a **fly**?		_____
8. Is it a **clock, crow,** or **clue**?		_____

Sounds and Sentences

Read each sentence. Circle the word that completes the sentence.
Write it on the line.

1. Cleo is a silly _____.	clown clock
2. She _____ like a hen.	clues clucks
3. She _____ her arms like wings.	flags flaps
4. Then she _____ a trick.	plays plods
5. She pulls an egg out of a clear _____.	glue glass
6. She cracks the egg on a _____.	play plate
7. A _____ pops out of the egg.	plant plead
8. The kids all yell and _____.	clap class

Name _____ Date _____

Match Pictures and Sentences

Read each sentence. Write the sentence that tells about the picture.

---

1. Fran plays the flute.
   Fran fixes a flat tire.

_____

- -

_____

2. Stan can dive and splash in the pool.
   Stan can drive to the store in his car.

_____

- -

_____

3. Greg plays lots of sports.
   Greg puts up the flag.

_____

- -

_____

4. The spider climbs in the web.
   The snake slides on the ground.

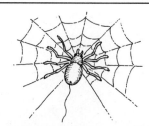

_____

- -

_____

Name _____ Date _____

Match Pictures and Sentences

Read each sentence. Write the sentence that tells about the picture.

1. A skunk sprays if it is scared.
   Steve scored the prize goal.

_____

- -

_____

2. Chris plants a tree.
   Chris grows big green plants.

_____

- -

_____

3. The baby plays with a stuffed frog.
   The baby in the crib is crabby.

_____

- -

_____

4. Cleo brushes and braids her hair.
   Cleo cleans the fruit she got.

_____

- -

_____

www.svschoolsupply.com

© Steck-Vaughn Company

Initial Blends Review

Phonics 2: Decoding, SV 6798-0

Word Hunt

Find the words in the box in the puzzle. Circle the words. The words may go across or down.

bridge	clap	crib	dry	frog
green	play	sleep	stop	try

```
C   L   A   P   L   A   Y

R   S   T   O   P   S   T

I   F   L   Z   X   L   R

B   R   I   D   G   E   Y

R   O   G   R   E   E   N

Z   G   P   Y   Z   P   Y
```

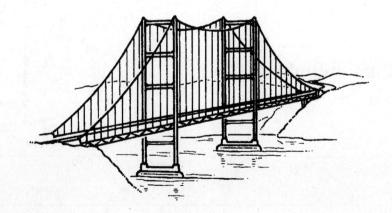

Name _____ Date _____

Hear and Write Final Blends

Name each picture. Listen to the last part of the word.
Write the last two letters.

ne**st**   de**sk**   wa**sp**   a**nt**   ju**mp**   ha**nd**

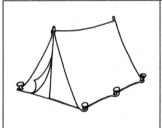         

_____   _____   _____   _____

_____   _____   _____   _____

_____   _____   _____   _____

Name _____   Date _____

Write Words with Final Blends

Name each picture. Circle the picture name. Write the name.

 want / wrist	 plant / plump	stamp / stand
 dent / dusk	 jump / just	 tent / test
 desk / dust	 band / bump	 stump / stand
 mask / nest	 wasp / wand	 mist / mask

www.svschoolsupply.com

© Steck-Vaughn Company

Final Blends

Phonics 2: Decoding, SV 6798-0

Riddles

Write a word from the box to answer each riddle.

bank	breakfast	damp	fast
stamp	stump	vest	west

1. It is a place to keep money. What is it? _____

2. You put it on a letter. What is it? _____

3. It is a meal. What is it? _____

4. It is the opposite of east. What is it? _____

5. It is a jacket with no sleeves. What is it? _____

6. It is a little bit wet. What is it? _____

7. It is what's left of an old tree. What is it? _____

8. It is the opposite of slow. What is it? _____

Sounds and Sentences

Read each sentence. Circle the word that completes the sentence. Write it on the line.

1. Randy can _____. _____	just jump
2. He can run _____. _____	fast faint
3. Today is the big _____. _____	test tusk
4. Is Randy the _____? _____	bunt best
5. Randy goes to _____ at the starting line.	stand stump
6. He runs by all the _____.	rest risk
7. He jumps _____ the best mark.	past plant
8. Randy is the _____.	chant champ

Match Pictures and Sentences

Read each sentence. Write the sentence that tells about the picture.

1. Jan has on the best mask.
   Jan has on pants and a vest.

_____

- - - - - - - - - - - - - - - - - -

_____

2. Mr. Rusk's tent pole has a big dent.
   Mr. Rusk takes the stumps off the land.

_____

- - - - - - - - - - - - - - - - - -

_____

3. The class cannot stand the band.
   The class gives the band a hand.

_____

- - - - - - - - - - - - - - - - - -

_____

4. The wasps fly into the nest.
   The ants crawl into the plant.

_____

- - - - - - - - - - - - - - - - - -

_____

Name _____   Date _____

Word Building

Follow the directions to build each word. Read each new word you
make. Write the last word to answer the question.

1. What **don't** you want on your car? _____
    Start with: **want**
    Change **a** to **e**: _____
    Change **n** to **s**: _____
    Change **w** to **v**: _____
    Change **s** to **n**: _____
    Change **v** to **d**: _____

2. Where do you keep a pet fish? _____
    Start with: **desk**
    Change **e** to **i**: _____
    Change **i** to **u**: _____
    Change **d** to **t**: _____
    Change **u** to **a**: _____
    Change **s** to **n**: _____

3. What is a good thing to keep in your bank? _____
    Start with: **hand**
    Change **h** to **l**: _____
    Change **a** to **e**: _____
    Change **l** to **b**: _____
    Change **d** to **t**: _____
    Change **b** to **c**: _____

Name _____ Date _____

Quiz Yourself

Name each picture. Fill in the circle next to the missing letters.
Write the letters.

 ○ mp ○ nt ○ sp ju____	 ○ nt ○ sp ○ st wa____	○ nt ○ st ○ sk ne____
 ○ nd ○ st ○ sk ba____	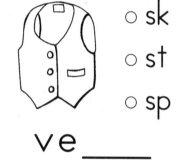 ○ sk ○ st ○ sp ve____	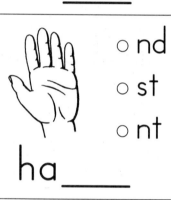 ○ nd ○ st ○ nt ha____
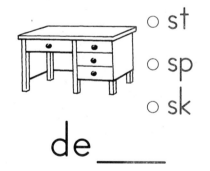 ○ st ○ sp ○ sk de____	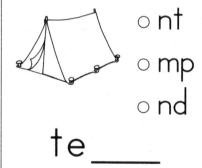 ○ nt ○ mp ○ nd te____	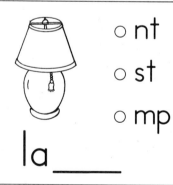 ○ nt ○ st ○ mp la____
 ○ st ○ nd ○ nt pla____	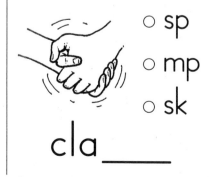 ○ sp ○ mp ○ sk cla____	 ○ st ○ sk ○ sp tu____

Quiz Yourself
Phonics 2: Decoding, SV 6798-0

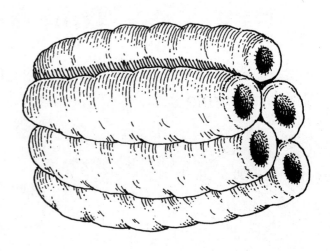

Most of us can't stand wasps. Wasps can sting. But wasps' nests are neat.

Many wasp families stay in the same nest. Some wasps use a very small stone as a tool.

What bug do you like? Draw it.

Wasps

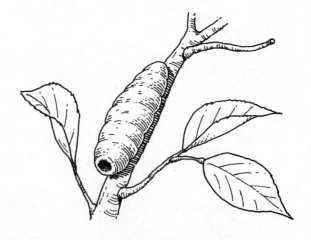

_____

made this book!

Hear and Write Digraphs ch and wh

Name each picture. Listen to the first part of the word. Write **ch** if you hear the same first sound as in **checkers**. Write **wh** if you hear the same first sound as in **whale**.

checkers

whale

Hear and Write Digraphs th, th, and sh

Name each picture. Listen to the first part of the word. Write **th** if you hear the same first sound as in **them** or **thumb**. Write **sh** if you hear the same first sound as in **shell**.

them   **th**umb   **sh**ell

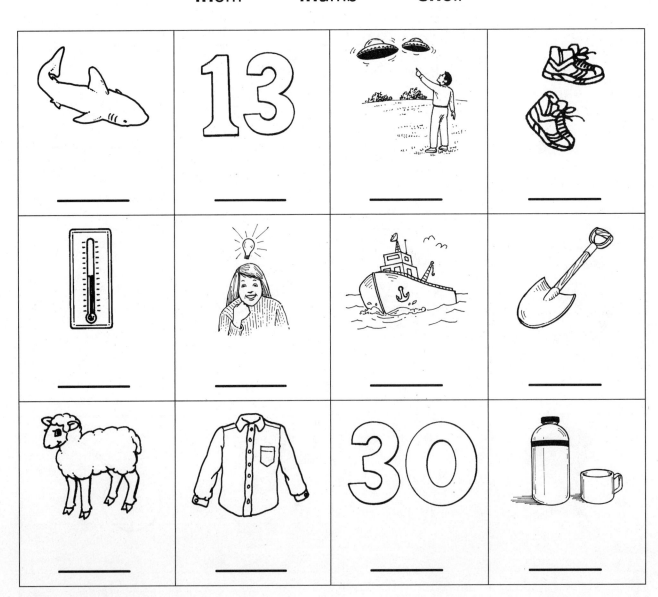

Write Words with Digraphs

Name each picture. Circle the picture name. Write the name.

chip sheep	chick shack	thorn when
share chair	shell whale	shirt third
cheese wheeze	chart shark	wheat cheat
thumb shame	them chin	wheel chill

Initial Digraphs Review

Phonics 2: Decoding, SV 6798-0

Name _____ Date _____

Sounds and Sentences

Read each sentence. Circle the word that completes the sentence. Write it on the line.

1. It's fun to go to the _____.	shore chore
2. You can look for _____ or go swimming.	shells wheels
3. If you swim, beware of _____.	sharks chats
4. They are not as big as _____.	cheese whales
5. But their teeth are as sharp as _____.	shoes thorns
6. Most of us do not need to fear _____.	third them
7. Sharks _____ away from people.	shy shin
8. _____ you see a shark fin, leave the sea.	White When

Initial Digraphs in Context

Phonics 2: Decoding, SV 6798-0

Crossword Puzzle

Use words from the box to complete the puzzle.

| wheat shirt chick them chart thorn |

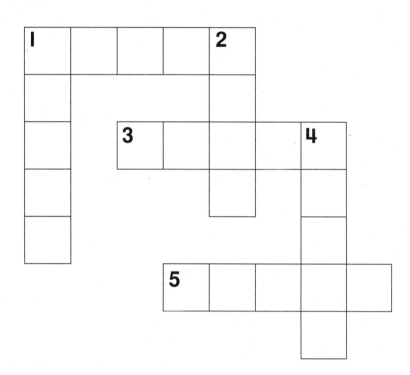

ACROSS

1.

3.

5.

DOWN

1.

2.

4.

Hear and Write Final Digraphs ch and th

Name each picture. Listen to the last part of the word. Write the last two letters.

bench   **tooth**

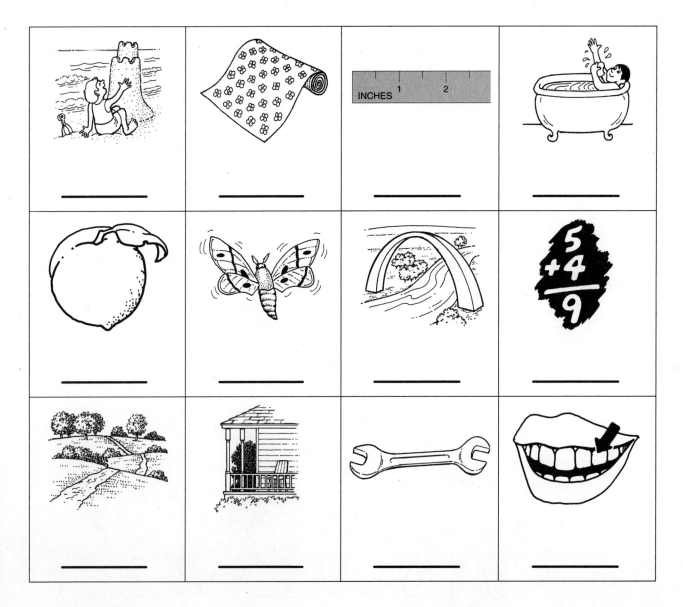

Name _____ Date _____

Hear and Write Final Digraphs
sh, ck, and tch

Name each picture. Listen to the last part of the word. Write the letters that stand for the last sound.

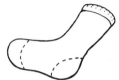

fish   **sock**   **watch**

www.svschoolsupply.com

© Steck-Vaughn Company

Final Digraphs **sh**, **ck**, and **tch**

Phonics 2: Decoding, SV 6798-0

Hear and Write Final Digraphs
ng and nk

Name each picture. Listen to the last part of the word. Write the last two letters.

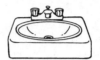

wing   **sink**

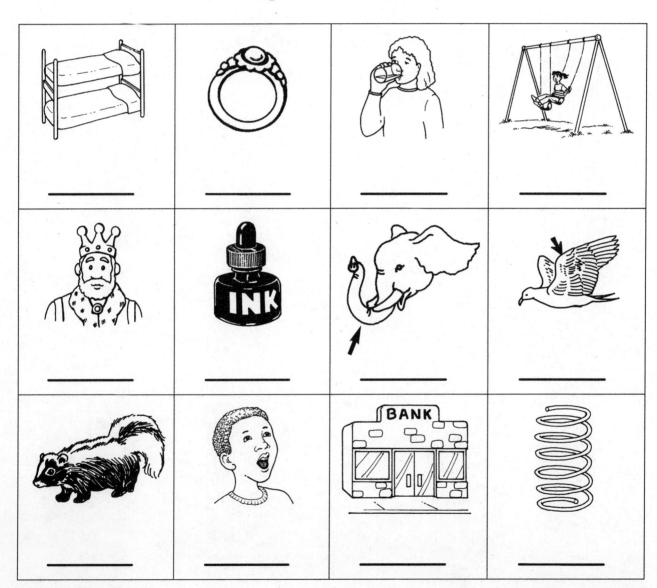

www.svschoolsupply.com

© Steck-Vaughn Company

Final Digraphs **ng** and **nk**

Phonics 2: Decoding, SV 6798-0

Name _____ Date _____

Write Words with Digraphs

Name each picture. Circle the picture name. Write the name.

ring rich	 clash cloth	 bench bank
tank tooth	shock skunk	 hang hatch
dish duck	 fang fish	 wash watch
 sink sock	porch path	 trunk track

www.svschoolsupply.com

© Steck-Vaughn Company

Final Digraphs Review

Phonics 2: Decoding, SV 6798-0

Sounds and Sentences

Read each sentence. Circle the word that completes the sentence. Write it on the line.

1. Life on a _____ can be hard.	tooth ranch
2. You must _____ the animals all the time.	watch skunk
3. You must keep cows out of the corn _____ .	patch peck
4. One chore is to _____ the horses.	math brush
5. There's not much time to rest on the _____ .	dish porch
6. There's no time to _____ in the spring.	fish math
7. You wish the dinner bell would _____ soon.	hatch ring
8. Then you crawl off to sleep in your _____ .	sink bunk

Words with Silent Letters in wr and kn

Name each picture. Listen to the beginning sound. If you hear **r,** as in **write,** write **wr.** If you hear **n,** as in **knight,** write **kn.**

write   **kn**ight

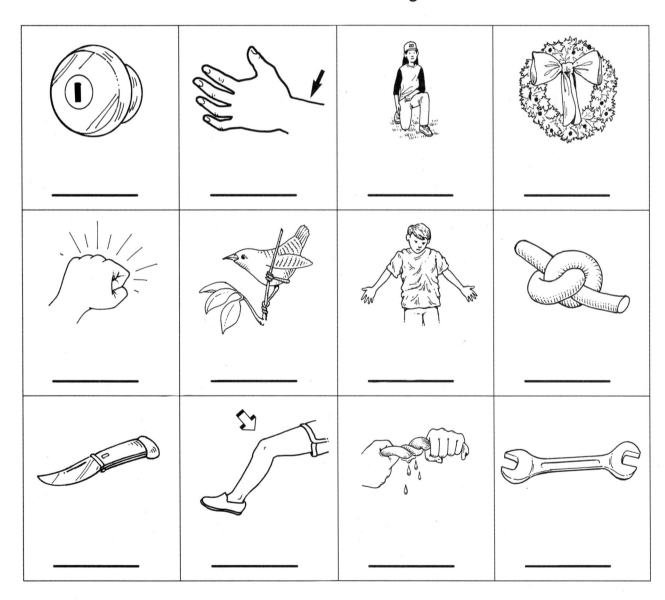

Write Words with Silent Letters

Name each picture. Circle the picture name. Write the name.

note knot _____ - - - - - - _____	week wreck _____ - - - - - - _____	whistle wrist _____ - - - - - - _____
knee need _____ - - - - - - _____	knit nice _____ - - - - - - _____	rent write _____ - - - - - - _____
red wrench _____ - - - - - - _____	knight nine _____ - - - - - - _____	neck knock _____ - - - - - - _____
knife kite _____ - - - - - - _____	rich wreath _____ - - - - - - _____	wren went _____ - - - - - - _____

Sounds and Sentences

Read each sentence. Circle the word that completes the sentence.
Write it on the line.

1. Did you ever _____ a scary story?	write itch
2. _____ of a scary first sentence.	Sing Think
3. "The _____ turned slowly."	knob bush
4. Go on _____ a scary setting.	with wash
5. "The _____ struck midnight."	clock porch
6. Add an odd noise, like a _____.	path screech
7. _____ as people read the story.	Watch Lock
8. See if they like what you _____.	wrote knot

Final Digraphs and Silent Letters in Context

Phonics 2: Decoding, SV 6798-0

Riddle Time

Fill in the circle next to the word that answers each riddle.

I. Where do strawberries grow?	○ tooth ○ thick ○ patch
2. What will hatch from a hen's egg?	○ thin ○ chick ○ shake
3. What do you hear when a hand hits a door?	○ thing ○ wrist ○ knock
4. How do you get an idea?	○ think ○ shine ○ sing
5. What sound can you make in water?	○ with ○ splash ○ clock
6. What is the name of a tool?	○ wrench ○ ring ○ path
7. What is the opposite of **us**?	○ mush ○ them ○ champ
8. What is the biggest living animal?	○ wren ○ wash ○ whale

Name _____ Date _____

Word Building

Follow the directions to build each word. Read each new word you make. Write the last word to answer the question.

1. What can you do with a bell? _____

    Start with: **knock**

    Change **kn** to **s**:   _____

    Change **ck** to **ng**:   _____

    Change **s** to **wr**:   _____

    Change **o** to **i**:   _____

    Change **wr** to **r**:   _____

2. What can you do with a ball? _____

    Start with: **fish**

    Change **f** to **w**:   _____

    Change **i** to **a**:   _____

    Change **sh** to **tch**:   _____

    Change **w** to **p**:   _____

    Change **a** to **i**:   _____

3. What can you do to your shoes? _____

    Start with: **chin**

    Change **n** to **p**:   _____

    Change **ch** to **wh**:   _____

    Change **wh** to **sh**:   _____

    Change **p** to **n**:   _____

    Add **e** at the end: _____

Quiz Yourself

Name each picture. Fill in the circle next to the missing letters.
Write the letters.

○ th ○ ch ○ ck ar___	○ ck ○ kn ○ wr __ench	○ sh ○ th ○ tch pa___
○ wr ○ kn ○ nk __ock	○ nk ○ ck ○ ng si___	○ wr ○ ng ○ kn __ite
○ kn ○ ng ○ nk __ee	○ nk ○ ck ○ th too___	○ th ○ ch ○ sh fi___
○ ch ○ ck ○ ng clo___	○ ck ○ th ○ ng ki___	○ wr ○ ng ○ kn __ot

Quiz Yourself

Phonics 2: Decoding, SV 6798-0

They stick in their heads. Now the ducks have the knack.

Mom must watch the baby ducks. She must teach them to fish. No! That's all wrong!

What did someone teach you? Write about it. Draw it.

Splish! Splash!

----

made this book!

_____
- - - - - - - - - - - - -
_____
- - - - - - - - - - - - -
_____

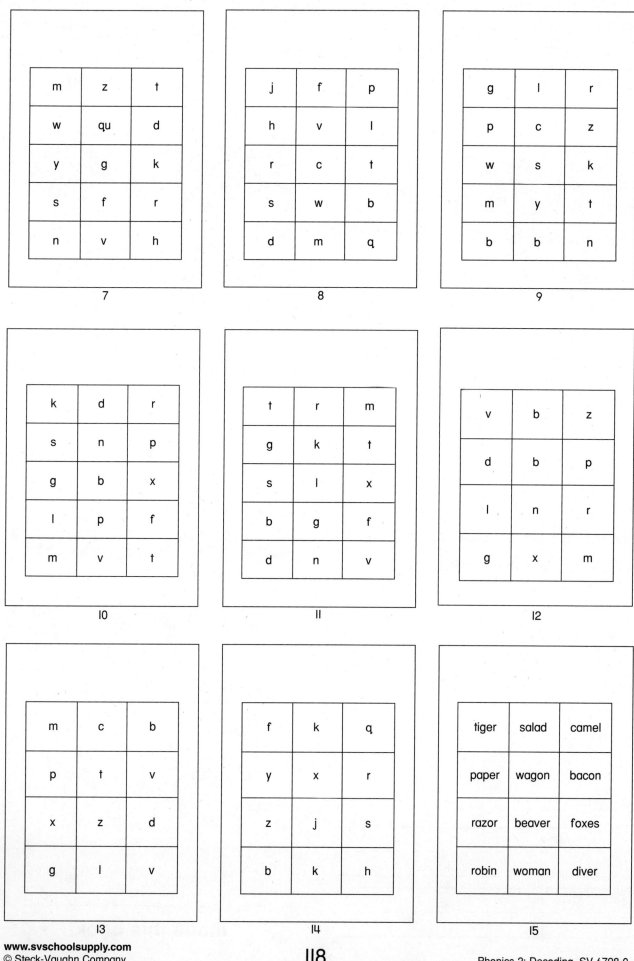

7

m	z	t
w	qu	d
y	g	k
s	f	r
n	v	h

8

j	f	p
h	v	l
r	c	t
s	w	b
d	m	q

9

g	l	r
p	c	z
w	s	k
m	y	t
b	b	n

10

k	d	r
s	n	p
g	b	x
l	p	f
m	v	t

11

t	r	m
g	k	t
s	l	x
b	g	f
d	n	v

12

v	b	z
d	b	p
l	n	r
g	x	m

13

m	c	b
p	t	v
x	z	d
g	l	v

14

f	k	q
y	x	r
z	j	s
b	k	h

15

tiger	salad	camel
paper	wagon	bacon
razor	beaver	foxes
robin	woman	diver

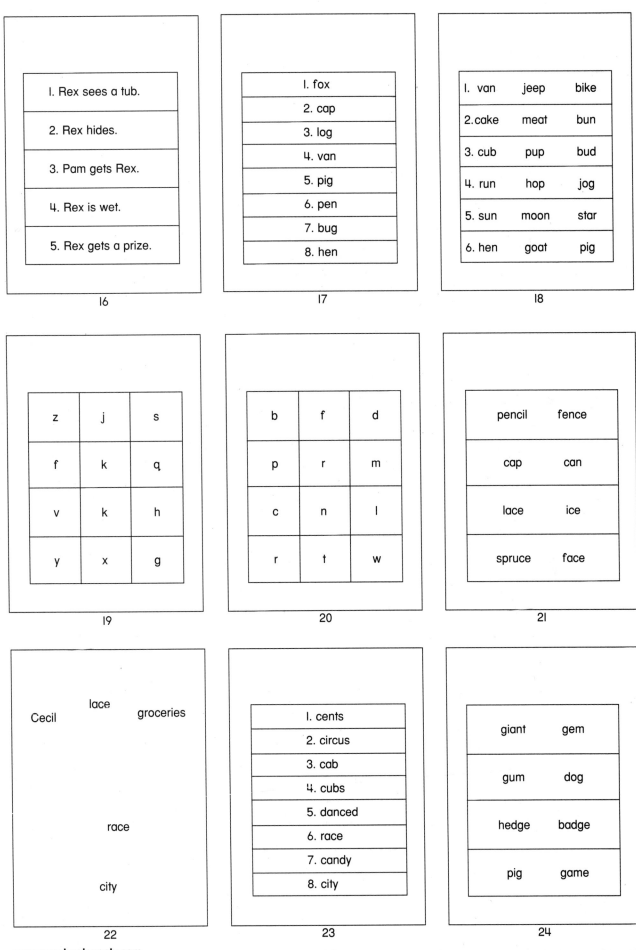

16

1. Rex sees a tub.
2. Rex hides.
3. Pam gets Rex.
4. Rex is wet.
5. Rex gets a prize.

17

1. fox
2. cap
3. log
4. van
5. pig
6. pen
7. bug
8. hen

18

1. van	jeep	bike
2. cake	meat	bun
3. cub	pup	bud
4. run	hop	jog
5. sun	moon	star
6. hen	goat	pig

19

z	j	s
f	k	q
v	k	h
y	x	g

20

b	f	d
p	r	m
c	n	l
r	t	w

21

pencil	fence
cap	can
lace	ice
spruce	face

22

Cecil   lace   groceries

race

city

23

1. cents
2. circus
3. cab
4. cubs
5. danced
6. race
7. candy
8. city

24

giant	gem
gum	dog
hedge	badge
pig	game

www.svschoolsupply.com
© Steck-Vaughn Company

Phonics 2: Decoding, SV 6798-0

25

1. giant
2. pig
3. gerbil
4. page
5. fudge
6. goldfish
7. hedge
8. stage

GIRAFFES

26

1. giant
2. gate
3. gym
4. giraffe
5. general
6. gas
7. gave
8. gem

27

s	z	sh
s	sh	z
s	z	s

28

sun	**rose**	**sugar**
see	wise	surely
seven	nose	tissue
us	music	mission
side	please	issue
gas	his	sure

29

1. surely
2. nose
3. rose
4. tissues
5. Please
6. sore
7. use
8. sure

30

1. Carmen sees the giraffe.
2. Sam soaps his car.
3. Gina goes to the sea.
4. The goat hops over a fence.

31

1. stage
2. car
3. game
4. judge
5. bus
6. nose
7. sugar
8. mice

33

a	a		a
	a	a	a
a	a		
a		a	a

34

bat	cat
bag	tag
cap	nap
ram	dam
fan	can

Phonics 2: Decoding, SV 6798-0

35

i		i	i
i	i		i
i		i	
	i	i	i

36

hill	mill
lid	kid
sit	hit
pin	fin
wig	pig

37

	o	o	o
	o	o	o
o	o	o	
o		o	o

38

rock	sock
sob	cob
ox	fox
cot	tot
mop	top

39

u		u	u
	u	u	u
u	u	u	
	u	u	u

40

sun	run
jug	bug
cub	tub
nut	hut
duck	luck

41

e	e		e
e	e		e
e		e	e
e	e	e	

42

cents	tent
bell	well
nest	vest
leg	beg
pet	net

43

mask	lamp	van
pen	vest	ten
bib	pig	king
sock	blocks	frog
drum	duck	rug

Phonics 2: Decoding, SV 6798-0

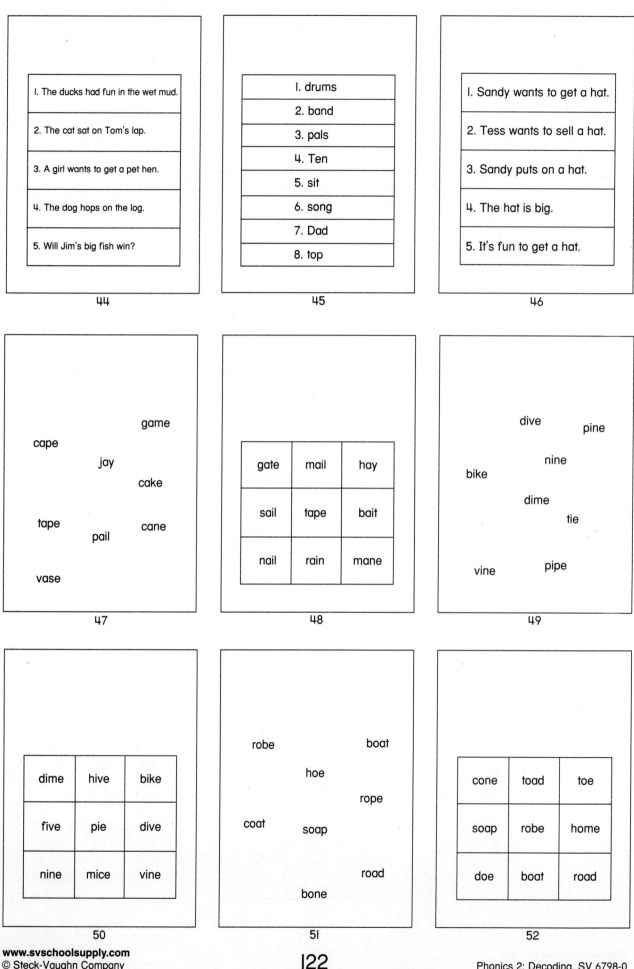

44

1. The ducks had fun in the wet mud.
2. The cat sat on Tom's lap.
3. A girl wants to get a pet hen.
4. The dog hops on the log.
5. Will Jim's big fish win?

45

1. drums
2. band
3. pals
4. Ten
5. sit
6. song
7. Dad
8. top

46

1. Sandy wants to get a hat.
2. Tess wants to sell a hat.
3. Sandy puts on a hat.
4. The hat is big.
5. It's fun to get a hat.

47

game
cape
jay
cake
tape   cane
pail
vase

48

gate	mail	hay
sail	tape	bait
nail	rain	mane

49

dive   pine
nine
bike
dime
tie
vine   pipe

50

dime	hive	bike
five	pie	dive
nine	mice	vine

51

robe   boat
hoe
rope
coat   soap
road
bone

52

cone	toad	toe
soap	robe	home
doe	boat	road

Phonics 2: Decoding, SV 6798-0

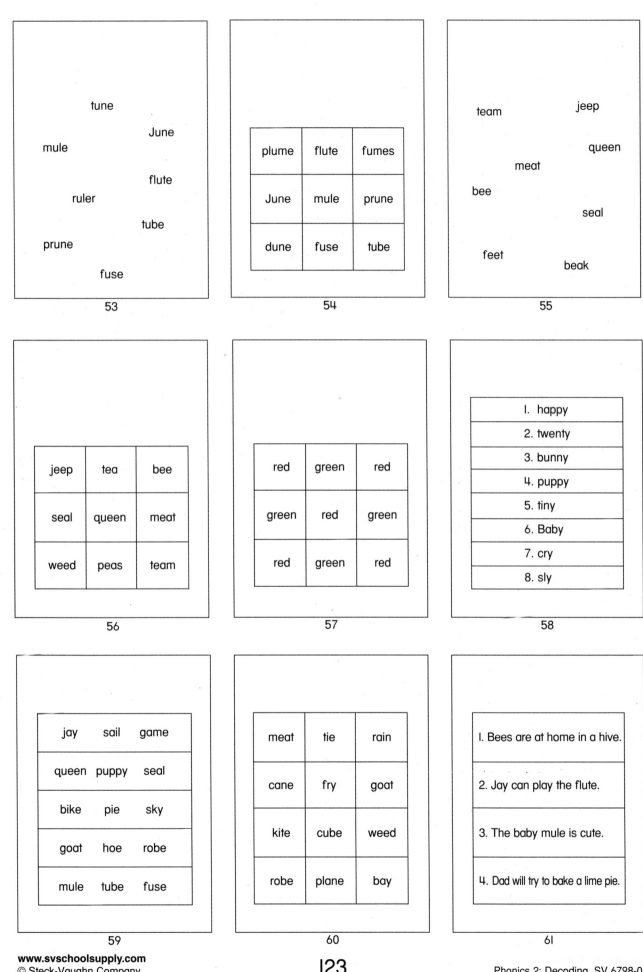

53

tune

June

mule

flute

ruler

tube

prune

fuse

54

plume	flute	fumes
June	mule	prune
dune	fuse	tube

55

team   jeep

queen

meat

bee

seal

feet

beak

56

jeep	tea	bee
seal	queen	meat
weed	peas	team

57

red	green	red
green	red	green
red	green	red

58

1. happy
2. twenty
3. bunny
4. puppy
5. tiny
6. Baby
7. cry
8. sly

59

jay	sail	game
queen	puppy	seal
bike	pie	sky
goat	hoe	robe
mule	tube	fuse

60

meat	tie	rain
cane	fry	goat
kite	cube	weed
robe	plane	bay

61

1. Bees are at home in a hive.
2. Jay can play the flute.
3. The baby mule is cute.
4. Dad will try to bake a lime pie.

Phonics 2: Decoding, SV 6798-0

62

Jean Hits a Home Run

63

box	sky	sail
mule	van	web
duck	five	bunny
hill	hoe	jeep

64

1. fly
2. trip
3. meet
4. pack
5. take
6. puppy
7. six
8. sky

65

barn

harp

star

shark

dart

yarn

arm   jar

66

thorn

stork   fort

torch

fork

porch

67

park	torch	star	porch
yarn	harp	horn	thorn
stork	cork	barn	arm

68

purse	twirl	fern
girl	stir	surf
skirt	nurse	shirt

69

surf	fork	shirt
girl	herd	barn
car	fern	bird
horn	scarf	church

70

1. hard
2. germ
3. stork
4. surf
5. twirl
6. barn
7. fern
8. girl

Phonics 2: Decoding, SV 6798-0

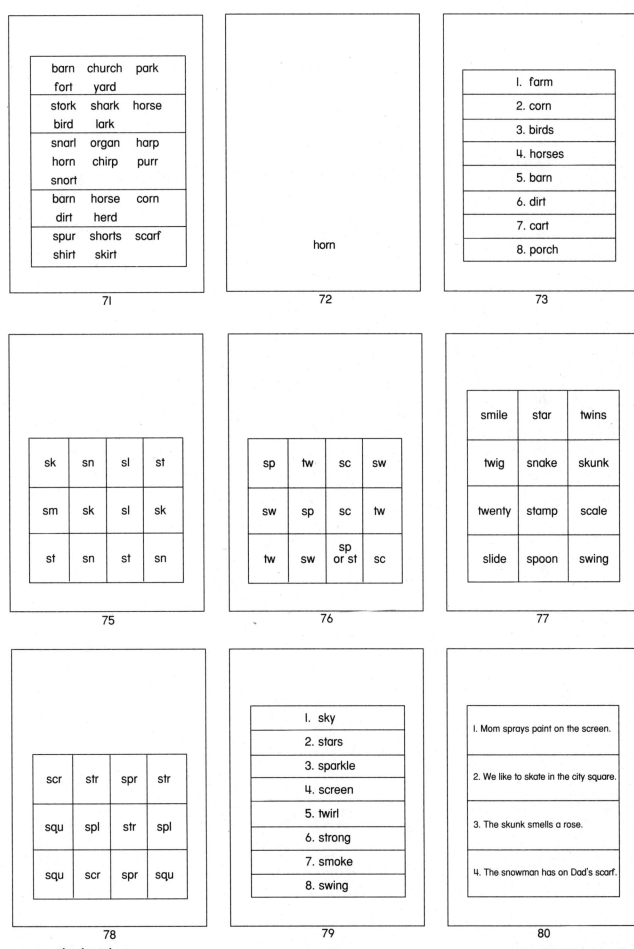

71

barn	church	park
fort	yard	
stork	shark	horse
bird	lark	
snarl	organ	harp
horn	chirp	purr
snort		
barn	horse	corn
dirt	herd	
spur	shorts	scarf
shirt	skirt	

72

horn

73

1. farm
2. corn
3. birds
4. horses
5. barn
6. dirt
7. cart
8. porch

75

sk	sn	sl	st
sm	sk	sl	sk
st	sn	st	sn

76

sp	tw	sc	sw
sw	sp	sc	tw
tw	sw	sp or st	sc

77

smile	star	twins
twig	snake	skunk
twenty	stamp	scale
slide	spoon	swing

78

scr	str	spr	str
squ	spl	str	spl
squ	scr	spr	squ

79

1. sky
2. stars
3. sparkle
4. screen
5. twirl
6. strong
7. smoke
8. swing

80

1. Mom sprays paint on the screen.
2. We like to skate in the city square.
3. The skunk smells a rose.
4. The snowman has on Dad's scarf.

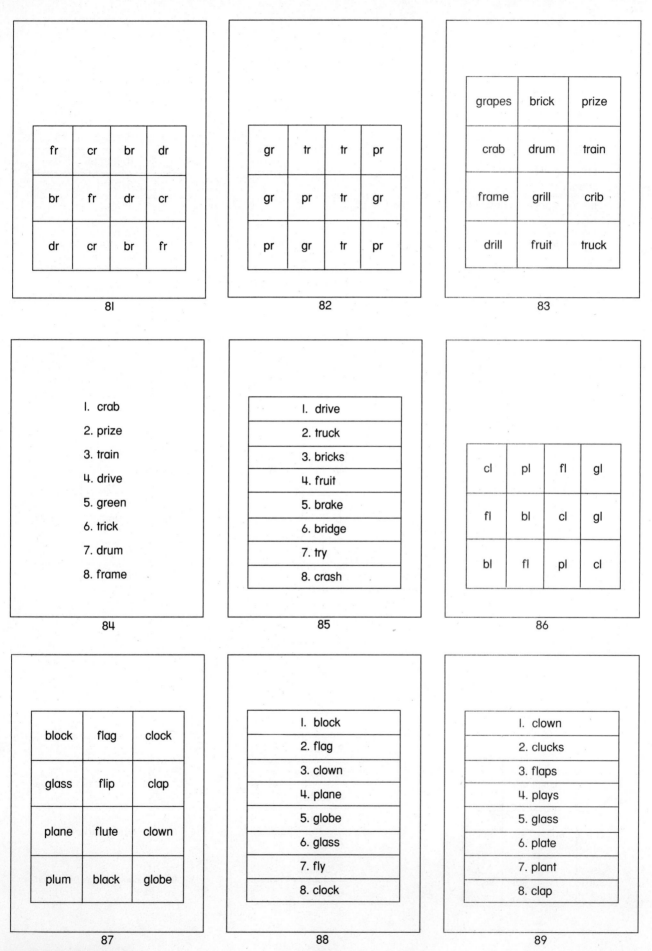

81

fr	cr	br	dr
br	fr	dr	cr
dr	cr	br	fr

82

gr	tr	tr	pr
gr	pr	tr	gr
pr	gr	tr	pr

83

grapes	brick	prize
crab	drum	train
frame	grill	crib
drill	fruit	truck

84

1. crab
2. prize
3. train
4. drive
5. green
6. trick
7. drum
8. frame

85

1. drive
2. truck
3. bricks
4. fruit
5. brake
6. bridge
7. try
8. crash

86

cl	pl	fl	gl
fl	bl	cl	gl
bl	fl	pl	cl

87

block	flag	clock
glass	flip	clap
plane	flute	clown
plum	black	globe

88

1. block
2. flag
3. clown
4. plane
5. globe
6. glass
7. fly
8. clock

89

1. clown
2. clucks
3. flaps
4. plays
5. glass
6. plate
7. plant
8. clap

Phonics 2: Decoding, SV 6798-0

90

1. Fran plays the flute.

2. Stan can drive to the store in his car.

3. Greg plays lots of sports.

4. The spider climbs in the web.

91

1. Steve scored the prize goal.

2. Chris grows big green plants.

3. The baby in the crib is crabby.

4. Cleo brushes and braids her hair.

92

```
C L A P L A Y
R S T O P S T
I F L A X L R
B R I D G E Y
R O G R E E N
Z G P Y Z P Y
```

93

nt	mp	sk	st
nd	nd	nt	st
nt	sp	mp	sk

94

wrist	plant	stamp
dent	jump	tent
desk	band	stump
nest	wasp	mask

95

1. bank
2. stamp
3. breakfast
4. west
5. vest
6. damp
7. stump
8. fast

96

1. jump
2. fast
3. test
4. best
5. stand
6. rest
7. past
8. champ

97

1. Jan has on the best mask.

2. Mr. Rusk takes the stumps off the land.

3. The class gives the band a hand.

4. The ants crawl into the plant.

98

1. DENT
went
west
vest
vent
dent

2. TANK
disk
dusk
tusk
task
tank

3. CENT
land
lend
bend
bent
cent

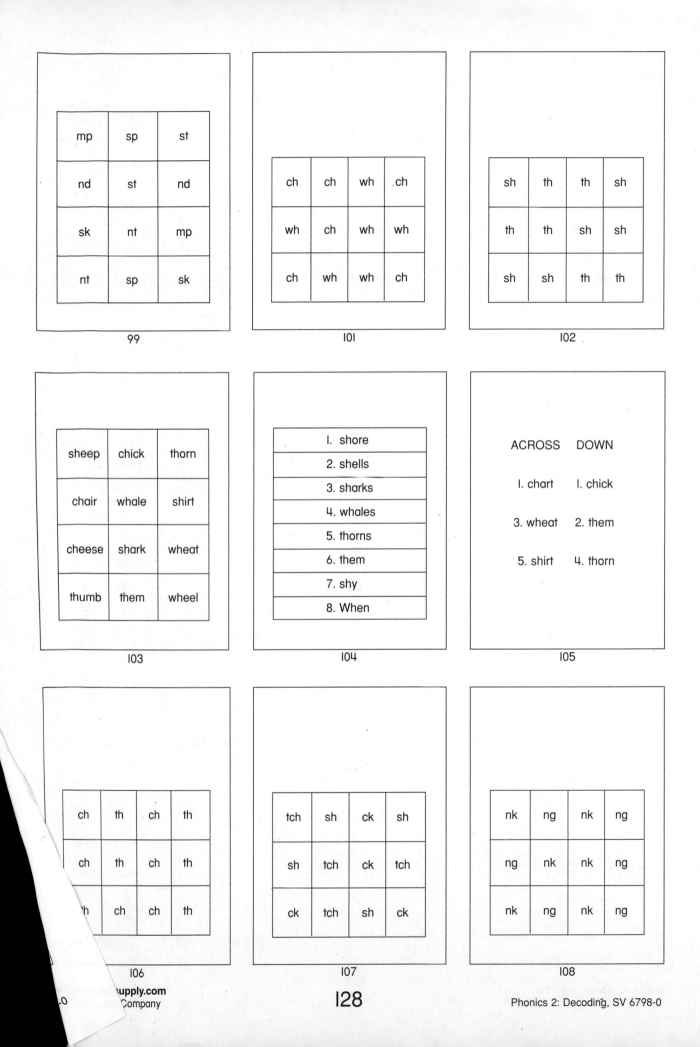

99

mp	sp	st
nd	st	nd
sk	nt	mp
nt	sp	sk

101

ch	ch	wh	ch
wh	ch	wh	wh
ch	wh	wh	ch

102

sh	th	th	sh
th	th	sh	sh
sh	sh	th	th

103

sheep	chick	thorn
chair	whale	shirt
cheese	shark	wheat
thumb	them	wheel

104

1. shore
2. shells
3. sharks
4. whales
5. thorns
6. them
7. shy
8. When

105

ACROSS	DOWN
1. chart	1. chick
3. wheat	2. them
5. shirt	4. thorn

106

ch	th	ch	th
ch	th	ch	th
'h	ch	ch	th

107

tch	sh	ck	sh
sh	tch	ck	tch
ck	tch	sh	ck

108

nk	ng	nk	ng
ng	nk	nk	ng
nk	ng	nk	ng

Phonics 2: Decoding, SV 6798-0